A Conversation with
Michael Pertschuk

A Conversation with Michael Pertschuk

Held on January 11, 1979
at the American Enterprise Institute for Public Policy Research
Washington, D.C.

ISBN 0-8447-3358-X

Library of Congress Catalog Card No. 79-3299

AEI Studies 255

Printed in the United States of America

Introduction

Michael Pertschuk has been chairman of the Federal Trade Commission (FTC) since April 1977 and has led the agency through one of its liveliest times in recent decades. No newcomer to Washington and no fainting heart, Mr. Pertschuk has reordered the commission's priorities and pressed his view that decisions be made on broader criteria than in the past. Undoubtedly, his most controversial move was proposing rules to place strict limitations on television advertising aimed at children.

Less specific and only slightly less controversial was his urging that social considerations, as well as traditional standards of competitiveness, be taken into account in antitrust decisions—a proposal that evoked criticisms from economists and businessmen alike. Decisions based on traditional grounds of enhancing economic or market efficiency have also been made under Chairman Pertschuk's leadership. For example, the FTC has struck down state laws barring advertising by optometrists and an FTC administrative law judge has found the American Medical Association's ban on commercial advertising by physicians to be unlawful. Also, following in the footsteps of his predecessors Lew Engman and Cal Collier, Mr. Pertschuk has been a strong advocate of deregulation of air and surface transportation.

Full disclosure has been another particularly important goal. For example, recent proposals would require funeral directors to notify bereaved families of the lowest priced coffin available. Others would require used-car salesmen to post the defects of their vehicles for prospective customers.

Some say this flurry of controversial regulatory initiatives is out of keeping with the present mood of the public. Mr. Pertschuk would appear to believe otherwise or in any event may plan to bring the public around to his point of view.

Mr. Pertschuk has had a long and distinguished career. After graduating from Yale Law School in 1959, he served as a legislative assistant to Senator Maureen Neuberger of Oregon (1962 to 1964), and went on to become chief counsel of the Senate Commerce Committee. While with the committee, Mr. Pertschuk became one of the congressional staff's most important and influential members. For example, he was instrumental in drafting numerous consumer protection measures, including the Magnuson-Moss Warranty—Federal Trade Commission Improvement Act. Ironically, the stringent standards for FTC rule making imposed by that act were the basis of a recent District of Columbia district court decision disqualifying Mr. Pertschuk from further participation in the children's advertising case. (He was said to have made prejudicial remarks on the subject.)

Among Mr. Pertschuk's published writings is an article that appeared in *Juris Doctor* in September 1974 entitled, "Getting Your Way in Washington." We are confident that he has much to offer on this and other subjects.

James C. Miller III
American Enterprise Institute

A Conversation with
Michael Pertschuk

I am delighted to be here and to see some old friends, to renew some acquaintances, and to go through some basic training for the new Congress. If my prognostications about the mood and interests of Congress are not mistaken, regulation is a topic of considerable concern.

Although often billed as such, the Federal Trade Commission (FTC) is not really a regulatory agency. Instead, it is primarily concerned with competition and making sure that the consumer regulates the marketplace through competition. While I will not pose this afternoon as a born-again economic conservative, I do think the agency, contrary to some public perceptions, can make a fair claim to a certain institutional humility. And that, although the learning curve of economic literacy for this commissioner may have been slow, there is evidence that it is on the rise.

I am delighted to see Cal Collier here because many of the most controversial, effective, and meaningful programs that the commission is working on represent a real continuity with the past. Seeds of perhaps as much as 80 or 90 percent of what we are doing were planted while Mr. Collier was there as general counsel, even before he became chairman. Thus, Cal cannot escape responsibility for what we are doing now. [Laughter.]

As I see it, the commission's primary business is competition, and our main purpose is to assure that the marketplace works. The mission of the Bureau of Competition, and even of the Bureau of Consumer Protection, has been to remove market restraints rather than to substitute governmental decision making for consumer decision making. We are seeking to improve the flow of information where the marketplace has failed to provide the consumer with the information that in turn enables him to act as the sovereign or disciplinarian of the marketplace.

Of course, we do not take the position that the more information the better, for information provision is not without costs. Instead, we aim to require producers to supply information only when the benefits of requiring such disclosures will substantially exceed the costs. And only when market forces alone cannot be relied upon to supply that information.

We are also trying to eliminate artificial barriers to the provision of information. Much of our work seeks to remove private restraints on the workings of the marketplace, especially those that prevent information from reaching consumers. The occupational licensure program is designed to eliminate such restraints, as well as artificial barriers to entry. This, I think, is an area in which we are in agreement with many of those associated with AEI.

As to competition, we are not ignorant of the importance of economies of scale. We are concerned, however, about the social costs of excessively large-scale enterprises, such as their distorting effect upon the political process.

We are also active in ferreting out areas of special interest regulation. We serve as competition advocates to eliminate forms of regulation designed to protect members of an industry against competition. For example, we have intervened before the Interstate Commerce Commission (ICC) and have played an active role before the Civil Aeronautics Board (CAB) and the International Trade Commission in seeking to restrain forces that would impair the marketplace through regulation.

Yesterday, when I visited Senator Thomas Eagleton, he expressed an idea of the commission which I think is fairly widespread—that of thousands of lawyers sitting around and, whenever more than one is idle, they get together and decide what to regulate next. Although, obviously, as with any image, there is a shadow of truth in this characterization, I am satisfied that the commission's actions are not haphazard nor are they based upon the excess energy of the staff. Instead, we have attempted to construct a decision-making apparatus that sets priorities. We seek to identify areas of substantial market failure and to find remedies that have some promise of producing benefits of substance. We are not interested in intervention for the sake of intervention nor the bringing of cases for the sake of winning them. The FTC is committed to making certain the consumer will be better off as a result of our activity.

Let me give an example of the difference between the way the

4

FTC, including the consumer protection people, approaches market problems and the ways other agencies sometimes approach them. The FTC has just finished a cooperative venture with the Department of Health, Education, and Welfare (HEW), which proposed a model state law to deregulate generic drug pricing. This project is one in which I think the commission can take just pride.

As you may know, pharmaceutical manufacturers have succeeded over the years in persuading state legislatures to restrict competition in the sale of multi-source drugs; that is, to eliminate the ability of the pharmacist to substitute a therapeutically equivalent generic drug for a brand name drug prescribed by a physician. We have proposed model legislation that allows a physician to insist upon a brand name drug by specifying "medically necessary" on the prescription if he feels the brand name drug is necessary. But, if he fails to do that, the pharmacist is free to determine whether to substitute a generic equivalent, and the price is free to respond to market forces. This recommendation, coupled with efforts to allow price advertising for drugs, will substantially stimulate competition in the sale of multi-source drugs.

The experience of Florida, where vigorous competition in the sale of generic drugs has broken out, indicates that the market does work. Several chains have been aggressive in advertising the sale of generic drugs. There is a high degree of substitution of generic drugs, and prices for the generic-substituted prescriptions run on average 32 percent less than brand name drugs. And pharmacists, under the pressure of competition, pass about 90 percent of the savings on to consumers, taking 10 percent as profit—the cost of their professional judgment.

Now, the institutional debate that arose between our staff people and some of the people at the Food and Drug Administration (FDA) is instructive. The FDA wanted the law to mandate the prescription of a generic substitute and a mandatory pass-through of all savings. Our study showed that in states that had mandated the pass-through, the law did not work. There were no police forces large enough to enforce it. Physicians and pharmacists resented it, and there were no economic incentives for pharmacists to find and stock the lowest-cost drugs. In effect, the debate pitted a lack of faith in the market against the belief that, if allowed to function without restraint, the market would provide the greatest benefits to consumers.

By dint of research and persuasiveness, we convinced HEW to follow our lead. Of course, we will continue monitoring the drug market to assure that the marketplace is allowed to function.

I think this example demonstrates, perhaps as much as any philosophical statement of commitment, that we really do have faith in the market when it is allowed to function.

Questions and Answers

DR. MILLER: I neglected to note at the onset that two of Chairman Pertschuk's associates, Bill Comanor and Bob Reich from the FTC are here today, and we also welcome them to AEI.

PAUL W. MACAVOY, Yale University: In the last few years, a great deal of high-quality economic research has been done in the Bureau of Economics of the FTC. The talented young authors there have contributed solidly to a set of findings that have become known as the "new learning" on the relationship between concentration in markets and noncompetitive performance. For a number of outside economists, the work of Dr. Qualls and Dr. Kwoka in particular, has disestablished any assumed relationship between high concentration and the usual aspects of noncompetitive performance, including high price/cost margins and excess profitability. I have heard that at one time cases were chosen at the FTC by asking the lawyers what they wanted to work on, but now the selection of cases involves the use of benefit-cost analysis in accord with the commission's established priorities. In view of this and the point I mentioned earlier, have you decided to disestablish the shared monopoly cases involving the large corporations in the cereals industry, in the energy industries, and in a number of other industries?

CHAIRMAN PERTSCHUK: This is very tricky to answer, partly because it involves cases in litigation before the commission. Let me note, however, that during my tenure no shared monopoly cases have been brought by the commission.

Frankly, I am more concerned about problems of market shares and dominant firms. On this topic I have been drawing upon the wisdom of Bill Comanor, of course, and Jeff Sheppard, whose work I find intriguing. In the search for new cases, the shared monopoly ones do not have as high a priority.

CALVIN COLLIER, American Enterprise Institute and former chairman, Federal Trade Commission: With the Line of Business victory, what is the prognosis for publication of research using those data, and how are those data coming in?

Chairman Pertschuk: I will let Bill Comanor answer that, but will preface his comments by saying that Ira Millstein, who represents the companies who lost the Line of Business case before the Supreme Court, says they may still launch an effort in Congress to have the Line of Business program circumscribed in some way.

William Comanor, director, FTC Bureau of Economics: The data for 1974 have just been received from all the companies. Unlike some other agencies, we are spending substantial amounts of resources auditing the numbers, going back to the companies to check them out, and making as certain as possible that the numbers reflect the true economic magnitudes.

We do not have all the data for 1975 and 1976, but given the efforts we are taking to assure the validity of the numbers, I think the best we could hope for is to have the data available for research work in the early fall. At that time we hope to start some economic studies using these data. We are beginning to work with some people in-house and will perhaps bring on some consultants to make use of what is perhaps the best economic data that have been available in some time.

Murray Foss, American Enterprise Institute: Could you explain a little more what types of studies you hope to make with the Line of Business data? Given the kinds of restrictions imposed by Congress and those you made after your battle with Congress, I am a little puzzled as to the kinds of things you can find out.

Dr. Comanor: The restrictions placed on the data have to do with confidentiality for the individual observations, but certainly not with the results of the analysis. Paul MacAvoy talked about some studies that have been carried out at the Bureau of Economics, and he and I agree that the data used in some of these earlier works have some problems. Thus, these studies are certainly not conclusive. I think that Professor MacAvoy would admit that we should not change public policy on the basis of these studies alone.

Certainly we hope to deal with some of the issues raised in studies by, say, John Kwoka, utilizing a much better source of information. More work on the relationship between market shares and profitability is something we want to see. We want to get away from the focus on concentration used in the past.

PROFESSOR MACAVOY: Kwoka's information in the new studies is based upon samples constructed from individual plant data.

DR. COMANOR: I think his data come from Environmental Impact Statement sources, although I am not certain. I think Dr. Kwoka would admit that, although the best available at the time, the data are less reliable than we hope the Line of Business data will be.

PROFESSOR MACAVOY: But it allowed him to do what the earlier census data disallowed because of confidentiality. That is, it allowed him to examine individually the top four firms in a four-digit industry definition and determine whether there was variation in their performance. He found, very interestingly, that the largest firms seemed to do much better than the second, third, and fourth largest. If this is true and if the firms are all charging about the same prices, is not the largest performing more efficiently and, therefore, improving the average for the four? The data that he had access to were precursors of the Line of Business data and did allow him to deal with individual decision-making units. If your confidentiality requirements are so strict that they put us back to where we were with the census data, we have not made progress.

DR. COMANOR: The individual investigator will be able to look at data for individual firms, by line of business, but the commission will clearly not publish the statistics on which the regression coefficients, for example, are based.

PROFESSOR MACAVOY: Will an investigator have to be certified as a Census officer, as he does to do research at the Census Bureau?

DR. COMANOR: No, he will simply have to be an employee of a certain division within the Bureau of Economics.

PROFESSOR MACAVOY: I think it unfortunate that the data will be restricted to government servants.

CHAIRMAN PERTSCHUK: I would be delighted to have you advocate the opening of these data, although we are committed to following through on our promise of confidentiality. It was the price to pay for getting the information.

Dr. Comanor: In reference to Kwoka's work, I would like to note my recollection that the market share of the second largest firm also had a substantial effect on industry profitability. This effect fell off after the top two firms.

Professor MacAvoy: Yes, the first one counted more than the second, and the second counted ten times more than the third.

Dr. Comanor: The first and the second, as I recall, were not that different, within the range of statistical certainty. Thus, a conclusion that only the first one counted would not be warranted as the basis of these results.

Dr. Miller: I have a question to which Senator Robert Griffin and Congressman Clarence Brown might also want to respond. From what I understand, this past year the FTC barely escaped having a legislative veto provision imposed by Congress—meaning that either house or both houses of Congress could have vetoed a regulation promulgated by the commission. The scuttlebutt from the Hill is that you may not escape next time. What are your views on this?

Chairman Pertschuk: I am not unsympathetic with the motivation for a legislative veto. I could not have worked for the Senate Commerce Committee for twelve years without sharing some sense of the frustration legislators have at what sometimes appears to be a bureaucracy gone wild.

I see the push for a legislative veto coming from two rather different sources. First, Congress feels a lack of control over the regulatory agencies. Second, those who would be the subject of regulation resist an agency's efforts to regulate and seek a perhaps more sympathetic forum.

Philosophically, we are the agents of Congress, and it is entirely appropriate for Congress to exercise a legislative veto. They can do so today through legislation and have moved rapidly when public outrage over such legislation as the auto seat belt interlock or the saccharin ban has arisen. I am primarily disturbed about the proposal for a single-house veto, which I oppose because it might lead to ill-informed decision making.

Also, I wonder if Congress is the proper forum for issues of such complexity. One of the most serious criticisms of the commission's rule making has been the length and the laboriousness of the process. But a benefit of that process has been that we have made our decisions with deliberation and on the basis of a solid record. We have had only three final rules under Magnuson-Moss to date. I think a poll even of those who are appealing them would show that the process was deliberate, that the rules were appropriately trimmed back, and that the record was responsive to the issues. That kind of deliberate process, built upon a record, is really not possible in a forum in which lobbyists for the affected industries will plead their cases in whispered conversations and a barrage of letters.

CONGRESSMAN CLARENCE J. BROWN (R-Ohio): What we have now is not legislative veto but veto by the committee that has oversight. For example, recently the Internal Revenue Service (IRS), under its legislative authority, proposed to deny the children of faculty members free tuition at educational institutions. The Ways and Means Committee, however, brought pressure on the IRS to rescind its policy— that rather than legislating the change.

My personal feeling is that the need for legislative veto springs from congressional inability to legislate in adequate detail. We leave many decisions open-ended, handing them to the regulators to determine, then Congress finds the result unsatisfactory. There has to be some means to restore to the legislative body that process of decision making and standard setting. The legislative process is flawed in that we do not take the time to work out in detail all that needs to be done. The function of the regulator is to flesh out the legislative idea.

Two of the worst examples are the Clean Air Act and the Occupational Safety and Health Administration (OSHA) legislation. Congress simply wanted occupational safety and health and left it to OSHA to work out the details. As the Clean Air Act has been amended, we are cleaning up details in that, too. But some of the early decisions by the regulators were not, in retrospect, what the Congress really intended.

PROFESSOR MACAVOY: Isn't that the definitive argument for the constitutionality of the one-house veto? That is, what Congressman Brown is saying, in effect, is that the Federal Trade Commission is delegated an extension of the legislative authority of Congress.

CONGRESSMAN BROWN: Which can be taken back.

Robert P. Griffin, American Enterprise Institute and former U.S. Senator from Michigan: Perhaps I can add a little political perspective to Congressman Brown's comment. In the recent election campaign I found an increasing demand in the country to do something about the mounting flood of regulation.

As I recall, when the Housing and Urban Development (HUD) legislation came through in the last session, the House adopted the one-house veto amendment. Although the Senate did not, there was a substantial support for it. My assessment is that, as a result of the last election, such an amendment will have more support in the Senate. It might be of some interest that one of the principal planks in my opponent's platform was to get a one-house veto to do something about all of these regulations.

Chairman Pertschuk: I had heard that. I gathered your opponent had initiated something like a legislative veto at the state level.

There is no question that the idea is gaining momentum. At the FTC we are seeking to winnow those aspects of proposed rules that cannot be justified. We want to make sure that the decision-making process is one that can inspire confidence that a rule is necessary and that the remedies are both appropriate and the least burdensome. The good they will do should substantially outweigh the cost. Whether we will succeed remains to be seen.

But I would not be surprised to see some form of legislative veto for all regulatory agencies emerge from this Congress. The President, of course, has an institutional concern over this issue, quite separate from that of the regulatory agencies. It is a question of the power of the presidency, especially with respect to the executive branch agencies.

Congressman Brown: May I turn this discussion to another subject? Circumstances and times change. The concern about monopoly in our society may be modified as our nation's position in the world changes. I have in mind trade relationships and, for instance, the problems of the steel industry in this country in competing with the nationalized steel industry of Japan.

We are no longer concerned only with internal trade but are looking to becoming more competitive as a nation in world trade. It is important to the future of our economy. We are competing with countries that establish a single national economic perspective; they may have two or three companies, but they are all controlled by a single national policy.

What ought our approach to that problem be from the congressional standpoint or from the regulator's standpoint? Should it be within the province of the regulator to modify anti-monopoly regulation and perhaps support a national monopolistic industry competing abroad, or should he continue to be responsive to the existing laws that in effect say break up those monopolies? Should it be the responsibility of Congress or the President to cite that problem and change the policy?

CHAIRMAN PERTSCHUK: The first step is to test the hypothesis, which is one of the things that I have asked Bill Comanor to do. Part of his responsibilities as director of the Bureau of Economics is to study the extent to which national cartels are essential in order to provide for a vigorous competitive effort abroad.

It is certainly a question that needs to be asked. Jim Adams, for example, has studied the policy of national champions in Europe. He has investigated whether picking a national champion, supported by an internal cartel, strengthens international competition. The results are not entirely clear on this question. So I think the first step is to raise and to study the question in more detail.

The issue also has to be addressed by Congress, where it is appropriate to reevaluate basic policies in the light of new study. But in direct response to your question, we must continue to respond to existing legislation; we have no choice.

JOHN W. BARNUM, attorney and former deputy secretary of transportation: I have a question about the commission's premerger notification program, specifically about one of the items in the reporting forms, which I propose as a candidate for a one-house veto, if the opportunity arises. The form requires the reporting company to submit, with its documentary response to the premerger notification, any memorandum its attorneys have prepared for its officers or directors that deals with market shares, and so forth. My understanding is that one of the premises of antitrust enforcement has always been that the most effective enforcers were, in fact, the private bar and the advice they give to their clients about what can or cannot be done. This requirement is one of the first instances that memoranda prepared by attorneys and delivered to their clients be disgorged in connection with looking at a merger.

In the early stages of consideration of a merger, this fact was called to the attention of half a dozen companies I know about, and everybody quickly backed off from writing something down. I am

concerned that in the long run the program is going to have a dele-
terious effect on private law enforcement and on educated decisions
about whether to attempt a merger. Surely the FTC can obtain more
reliable information about things such as market shares from outside
counsel and from surveys and analyses than the legal opinions that
the lawyers may hand to a company's board of directors.

Has the commission considered amending the requirement so
that attorneys could give such memoranda to their clients without
having these documents turned over if the corporation goes ahead
with the merger?

CHAIRMAN PERTSCHUK: That issue has not been raised recently, and I'll
take a look at it.

MR. BARNUM: How about the premerger notification program as a
whole?

CHAIRMAN PERTSCHUK: I think it is generally working well. We feel
we are generally getting the initial notices and the data. The program
has not produced a great profusion of new cases, but Sandy Pfunder,
who is running the program, reports that we are getting the information, and analysis is being performed. It is too early to tell much, but
it seems to be working.

ROBERT B. REICH, director, FTC Office of Policy Planning and Evaluation: Let me add that there will be an ongoing evaluation of the program.

CHAIRMAN PERTSCHUK: Yes, we are committed to a year-end review of
the premerger rules to see how they worked and to look at questions
which were not resolved.

PROFESSOR MACAVOY: Considering the Engman-Collier-Pertschuk output and the model operating practices of the commission, I might go
so far as to assert that its job is done—that the commission has succeeded in making the American economy competitive, well informed,
and efficient. However, the head of the antitrust division of the Department of Justice spoke at an AEI discussion a few weeks ago and
had a laundry list of things remaining undone by the FTC and by his
agency. Do you have such a list?

CHAIRMAN PERTSCHUK: I have tried to spell out in some of my statements and in some of our reports things that I think are undone, and it is a long list. We are a very modestly sized agency. Our budget would run HEW for only forty-five minutes. [Laughter.]

With these modest resources we can make a contribution to ensuring competition. There is much to be done in the area of private restraints.

Among the programs that Cal Collier initiated that have great potential are those calling for some element of competition in health care. We are not advocating substantially more regulation of the health industry. We are, I think, the preeminent voice arguing for competition in health care delivery. We are also reviewing professional restraints. The area of professional qualifications and specialization is, of course, an extremely delicate one. We are not about to overrule the decisions of the medical schools as to who should practice medicine. On the other hand, we are investigating the extent to which physician dominance of Blue Shield boards represents an inherent conflict of interest. We are questioning whether it affects who gets paid and how much and related issues.

Professor MacAvoy: Your response is interesting, because it says the FTC will do much the same as now, perhaps thrusting into the service sector of the economy in which its previous activities have not been so extensive—an area that is rather far afield.

What about the structure and performance of American industry? It has not become more concentrated. It has not developed new practices of cartelization to meet foreign competition. There are no signs of manifest anti-competitive behavior. The FTC is as unable to find any electrical conspiracies now as it was twenty years ago. Within the heart of your territory, the commission seems to have done it all.

Chairman Pertschuk: I think not. We are concerned about the current merger wave. We have been working with John Shenefield and his Antitrust Division and also Senator Ted Kennedy's committee in looking at the conglomerate merger situation. We consider it troublesome, not as a matter of economics, but as a matter of the increased concentration of economic power. We have addressed, in a preliminary way, our concerns about the nature of the current conglomerate wave, and we will be working on legislative proposals in this area.

We also participated in the National Commission's [1] deliberations

---

[1] National Commission for the Review of Antitrust Laws and Procedures.

on persistent monopoly power—dominant market share over a period of time. We advocated a form of no-conduct monopolization as an amendment to the Sherman Act.

In looking at conglomeration, we are aware of the value of the conglomerator in disciplining inefficient management. Instead of a flat ban on acquisitions by the very largest companies, we have been investigating some form of cap or spin-off requirement. Acquisitions would be allowable, but only with a concurrent spin-off.

PROFESSOR MACAVOY: The interest of the commission and its cousin in conglomeration seems to be highly cyclical. Is it fair to say that when the great recession of 1980 occurs, I need not worry about your interest in conglomeration?

CHAIRMAN PERTSCHUK: I suggest we both wait. [Laughter.]

MR. COLLIER: Chairman Pertschuk, you mentioned earlier your increased concern about dominant firms. I assume that might mean two-firm industries as well, in light of the research you mentioned. Apart from your suggestion of legislation to revise the monopolization standards, what implications would this concern have for your enforcement policies?

CHAIRMAN PERTSCHUK: I am intrigued by an issue you raised before leaving the commission: the possibility of imposing duties upon a monopolist. We have set up a task force to look at remedies short of divestiture and spin-off.

MR. COLLIER: So that a behavior approach would possibly be implied by that observation? But from an enforcement standpoint, what kind of case selection possibilities or other visible evidence of your concern will there be in the near future? The one thing that seems to be missing in this debate is a coherent theory of the evolution of the dominant firm. I am wondering what kind of enforcement approach would be taken, since many firms find themselves dominant in an industry, and it is a matter of considerable interest to them.

CHAIRMAN PERTSCHUK: It is too early to say. We will await the presentation of theories and cases by the Bureau of Competition.

MR. COLLIER: I suspect that further research may explain some of the conglomeration as well. As firms become very successful in particular industries, they conglomerate, rather than staying in their own industry, in order not to attract the attention of enforcement officials who are too preoccupied with the last 5 percent market share.

RODERICK HILLS, attorney and former chairman, Securities and Exchange Commission: Chairman Pertschuk, you have been justly credited with trying to organize the priorities of your agency. Where on your list do you place existing government regulations and laws—not necessarily FTC's—that are obviously anti-competitive?

CHAIRMAN PERTSCHUK: Quite high. On the other hand, we do not want to duplicate the efforts of agencies that are already fully involved. For example, we were active before the CAB, but the CAB has now gained sufficient momentum so that it does not need help from the FTC. With respect to the ICC, we have a modest commitment of resources, but the Justice Department also has a very substantial commitment. We have a substantial allocation for the Energy Department and some of its regulations. And Fred Kahn has asked us to help him look at the anti-competitive impact of state regulation, which is to a large extent an unexplored field.

CONGRESSMAN BROWN: Who has the authority to undertake action on state regulation?

CHAIRMAN PERTSCHUK: Sometimes we have; it depends upon the nature of the regulation. We have broad authority to study the behavior of the marketplace, quite apart from our enforcement responsibilities. For example, in the area of insurance we have only limited enforcement authority because of the McCarran-Ferguson Act, but our authority to study the behavior of the market and to make recommendations to the public and to Congress does encompass insurance. We have studied the adequacy of regulations of life insurance cost disclosure and of private insurance to supplement income.

Generic drug price disclosure is an area in which we might have had authority to issue a preemptive rule. Instead of trying to preempt state laws, however, we chose to work with the states to develop a model law, which we offered to them for consideration.

We are not looking for conflict with state regulators. On the other hand, our basic statute deals with restraints of trade. The applicability of *Parker* v. *Brown* to the FTC and the extent of FTC preemptive authority over state regulation are relatively unsettled. The first test probably will be a court decision on our preemptive action

in the eyeglass rule, in which we sought to free opticians from restraints against advertising. In many cases restraint is enforced by
state law.

Mr. Hills: What is being done about *federal* laws that restrict advertising in some industries?

Chairman Pertschuk: We have advocated that the Bureau of Alcohol,
Tobacco, and Firearms (BATF) not restrain responsible price and
quality competition in the sale of alcoholic beverages.

Mr. Hills: The Security and Exchange Commission (SEC) regulates
that industry by prohibiting certain kinds of advertising. But back to
the FTC, does going after these things really have high priority?

Chairman Pertschuk: Yes. Many of the restraints, of course, have
been private. The temptation of the voluntary advertising review
boards and codes of professional conduct has always been to restrain
the vigor of comparative advertising. We have investigated them in
the past and have counseled the boards to tread very gingerly on sup-
pressing vigorous comparative advertising.

   We have also intervened with the BATF but have no authority to
require them to do anything. If the SEC is inappropriately suppress-
ing competition, we would like to know about it.

Mr. Hills: Will you seek legislation to change the laws with respect
to the BATF, for example?

Chairman Pertschuk: In regard to BATF, it is a question of interpret-
ing the law. Secretary Blumenthal has undertaken a reevaluation of
their regulations with an eye toward freeing up competition.

Mr. Hills: In a sense, what is being done by the administration's
Regulatory Analysis Review Group could be done very efficiently by
a task force at the Federal Trade Commission—picking out targets
and going after them in a conscientious way. There are a lot of tax
laws, for example, that obviously discriminate against some important
forms of capital. Are you looking into this area?

Chairman Pertschuk: Yes. Bob Reich has a task force looking at the
possible anti-competitive impact of the tax laws.

Mr. Hills: Tax laws seem to be at the base of the kinds of conglomerate mergers that you are worried about. Why not look there instead of at the effects of mergers?

Chairman Pertschuk: Indeed, we have been looking at the impact of tax laws as initiators of conglomeration.

Senator Griffin: It seems obvious that tax laws have a lot to do with the concentration of ownership in the media, particularly newspaper chains. As I recall, the FTC had a seminar on the subject not too long ago that attracted quite a lot of attention. Has there been any follow-up?

Chairman Pertschuk: There was a curious reaction to the seminar, because concentration in the media is such a sensitive subject. The FTC has authority over mergers in the media, except for television and radio. We had a number of complaints, one from the Authors' Guild, against some specific mergers in book publishing and newspaper publishing.

Looking into some of the complaints, we found two clearly competing public policies reflected in the First Amendment and the antitrust laws. On the one hand, the antitrust laws clearly show concern about excessive concentrations of power, and, with respect to the media, the desirability of maintaining multiple outlets is enhanced by the First Amendment's concern for free speech. On the other hand, any effort by a government agency, even one designed to enhance competition, is a form of intervention which carries the threat of chilling speech.

Our decision was not to take the enforcement route initially. Instead, we utilized our authority and responsibility to study a trend among the media which is clearly troubling to many people. We are reserving judgment until we have analyzed not only the papers given at the conference but also the response to them from others.

We might have handled the situation better, but we were exercising institutional restraint in not opening up a series of investigations that would have led to complaints. We want to understand the nature of what is happening and its implications before we undertake to challenge any specific mergers. There are strong arguments that, in some cases, group ownership of newspapers provides greater editorial independence and stability than that enjoyed by the fragile single-family newspaper. It is very difficult to get proof that vertical integration in publishing reduces the opportunity for new authors to get printed. These issues are very elusive, and there will be no clear answers for some time.

Mr. Reich: As for the tax question, we have spent the last six months with a few economic public finance consultants trying to get a sense of the interrelationship between tax policy and competition. We were amazed to discover that very few people have given much thought to the subject—it falls between the academic and analytic cracks. We hope that in six to eight months we will be in a position to highlight, perhaps in a report to Congress, some of the critical problems in that area.

Chairman Pertschuk: On the question of media ownership and the tax consequences, Congressman Morris Udall has sponsored a bill that deals with the estate tax consequences of passing on family-owned newspapers. That will be one of the pieces of legislation we will try to apply some of our knowledge to.

Arthur F. Burns, American Enterprise Institute and former chairman, Federal Reserve Board: The Federal Trade Commission has been around for a good many years. What major contributions has it made to creating or maintaining a healthy competitive environment in this country? Or, to put the same question another way, if the commission were abolished today, would we have a very different world?

Chairman Pertschuk: In the area of competition the commission, for better or worse, has probably substantially retarded the pace of horizontal merger activity over the last couple of decades.

In the area of consumer protection the commission, together with voluntary restraints that resulted from its active presence, has succeeded in improving the flow of information through truth in advertising. I think the claims of national advertising today are probably as adequately substantiated as they have ever been, which is helpful, not only to consumers, but to the integrity of the marketplace. The commission as a source of independent advice to Congress on economic measures has been, and can continue to be, an effective watchdog for the impact of proposals on consumers and on competition. Also, the Bureau of Economics has done significant work in the past, which I think will continue.

But I would have to say that the commission cannot claim any great credit for reshaping the structure of this economy.

Field Haviland, American Enterprise Institute: Couldn't you make an even stronger case by pointing up your connections with other regulatory agencies which work along the same lines, such as the Food and Drug Administration and the SEC? It seems to me that truth in advertising and reasonable conditions of competition are the result not only of your agency's efforts but of its cooperation with other agencies.

Mr. Hills: Then we would have to ask about the justification of the other agencies. [Laughter.]

But on another subject, what will you say on the Robinson-Patman Act?

Chairman Pertschuk: Of course, I cannot comment on cases which we have brought, but we find that with judicious case selection there is an appropriate and economically justifiable role for the Robinson-Patman Act.

Professor MacAvoy: You have no plans to seek amendment of it?

Chairman Pertschuk: No.

Professor MacAvoy: Returning to Dr. Haviland's point, an American Bar Association (ABA) commission report has suggested that there is too much competition among agencies in this area and that it is wasteful, duplicative, and inefficient. Would it be possible to divest the FTC of those activities of which you are proud and put them in the Antitrust Division of the Department of Justice? Wouldn't that reduce the expenditure of federal dollars for agency activities and maybe increase the quality of output a little because the staff at the Antitrust Division is better than at the Federal Trade Commission? [Laughter.]

Chairman Pertschuk: I, of course, do not agree with your assessment of the FTC staff. Nor do I agree that there has been duplicative and overlapping work. Whatever the arguments for a super agency, the working relationship between the Justice Department and the FTC is one of coordination, not duplication. There is no chance that we will waste resources by both investigating the same thing. I think the transactions costs of having the two agencies are quite low, and there are benefits.

Mr. Collier: You have mentioned your political and social concerns with the size of corporations or of a few corporations in combination. A common criticism is that there are no objective standards to indicate at what level your concern will evoke some kind of government response. How do you address this criticism? At what size do bells go off for you as a government official and call for enforcement measures?

Chairman Pertschuk: We have taken the position that this issue should be addressed legislatively.

Professor MacAvoy: Do you think Congress, with a staff of 11,000 analysts, is prepared to tell when concentration is too high?

David Boies, Chief Counsel of Senate Judiciary Committee: The Senate, with only 6,000 analysts, is preparing some legislation in that area. It will at least open the debate as to when, through merger and acquisition, companies begin to exceed the size required by efficiency and begin to raise social and political problems that tend to accompany the concentration of any kind of power in a democracy.

Professor MacAvoy: Professors Carl Kaysen and Donald Turner say concentration is too high when the top eight firms have 60 percent of the market.[2]

Mr. Boies: We are not talking about concentration within a particular market. We are talking about a base of economic power that carries with it social and political power. The Fortune 500 firms account for something like 83 percent of all of the manufacturing and mining assets in the country, an increase of more than 15 percent in the last ten years and of more than 20 percent in the last two decades. That is a fairly significant increase and a fairly significant concentration of economic power.

Professor MacAvoy: Concentration of assets but not of economic power?

Mr. Boies: That depends on what is meant by power. Revenues have had a similar increase in concentration; in terms of profits, the in-

---

[2] *Anti-Trust Policy: An Economic and Legal Analysis* (Cambridge, Mass.: Harvard University Press, 1959).

crease in concentration among the Fortune 500 firms has even been greater.

PROFESSOR MACAVOY: You mean profits have gone up more rapidly than wealth acquisition? That suggests there may be additional efficiencies in the large-scale firms.

MR. BOIES: I said revenues have gone up as assets have gone up. Profits have gone up more rapidly than revenues.

PROFESSOR MACAVOY: That sounds like quite an accomplishment. You have already argued that concentration is unchanged within relative markets.

MR. BOIES: No, I said the two were independent. There are certainly markets in the United States where concentration has increased. There may also be markets in the United States where concentration has decreased. Whether the increase or decrease of concentration in particular markets has affected profits in those markets is inconclusive.

PROFESSOR MACAVOY: But if this increased concentration in revenues has not been accompanied by an increase in economic power, the increase in profitability must have come from a reduction in costs.

MR. BOIES: Not at all. If a company has more assets and more revenues and more employees and more profits, it has more economic power. It has power to affect the kinds of decisions people have to live with. We are not talking about economic power in terms of market share.

DR. BURNS: You are discussing the Fortune 500. Do you have information on the top 100, the top 50, or the top 10?

MR. BOIES: As I recall, the top 100 went from approximately 38 percent in 1965 to approximately 43 percent in 1975.

MR. HILLS: Most of that increase was a redefinition that brought in two or three very large companies.

MR. BOIES: I don't think so. Do you mean by "redefinition" that different companies have been brought into the Fortune 500? It may be true of the top 50, but it is also true of the top 200. In terms of the percentage of total assets in the economy the increase in concentration in the last fifteen years has been greatest in the second 100 within the 500, followed by the third, fourth, and fifth hundreds. The increase has been less within the top 100, and the top 50.

Dr. Burns: Analyzing the figures that way might lead to a different conclusion about economic power. Have these analyses been published?

Professor MacAvoy: In a recent volume, Charles Berry essentially made these calculations for the earlier Fortune issues.[3] His study backed up the claim that the turnover within the top 100 firms was very rapid. Plants were bought and sold at such a rate that essentially half the sample were owned by firms that did not own them five years before. The growth rate in the second 100, however, was much higher. Berry concluded that the Darwinian processes were really increasing, not reducing, competition.

Chairman Pertschuk: Let me mention in this regard one economy of scale, and that is lobbying. The ability to attract the best lobbying talent is a function of larger scale.

Congressman Brown: Another economy of scale follows directly: the ability to respond to government regulations. Unfortunately, many small businesses are not able to cope as well as their large competitors are. American Motors and Chrysler are great examples with respect to their difficulty in meeting fuel consumption and clean air requirements. Are you addressing the problem of how government regulation affects concentration of economic power?

Mr. Hills: And, does this argument not suggest that the commission's Bureau of Economics should pay more attention to what has caused the levels of concentration in the Fortune 500 rather than emphasizing existing levels?

Chairman Pertschuk: The heart of the issue is not economic research or the growth patterns of the top 50 or 100 or 200 companies in the last twenty years. The issue is fundamental Jeffersonian democracy. It is an essential distrust of substantial concentrations of power. Cal

---

[3] Charles H. Berry, *Corporate Growth and Diversification* (Princeton: Princeton University Press, 1975).

Collier raises a valid point—that these questions of political and social implications have not been addressed with the same intellectual rigor as questions of economic concentration.

CONGRESSMAN BROWN: Consider the inability of American Motors and Chrysler to respond to the Clean Air Act, the Highway Traffic Safety Act, and all the other pieces of legislation addressed to the automobile industry since 1965. The point has been reached where only General Motors—and, in some areas, Ford—is able to deal with the requirements government has imposed.

CHAIRMAN PERTSCHUK: The question is valid, but I'm not sure that behavior bears out the hypothesis. Not only Ford and GM, but Honda and Volvo and some other companies that are very small compared even to American Motors and Chrysler have been able to respond very well and competitively to those regulations.

I agree that the early consumer protection legislation of the 1960s failed to take account of the different competitive impact of regulation on smaller and larger firms. Some of that regulation may have had an unintentional anticompetitive impact. As part of the process of evaluating proposed rules, we are taking into account what the impact will be on smaller firms.

DR. BURNS: Do you know if that has been done for the automobile industry?

CHAIRMAN PERTSCHUK: I suspect that the National Highway Traffic Safety Administration has addressed that issue, but I am unfamiliar with the specific work they have done.

AUSTIN RANNEY, American Enterprise Institute: When economists and lawyers get to wrangling about specifics, I have a tough time seeing the forest for the trees. So I want to go back to a very large, sloppy question about the legislative veto that nobody really knows the answer to.

At a conference AEI held a couple of weeks ago, a former representative from Michigan, Jim O'Hara, was asked about the legislative veto. He was one of the members of Congress who had pushed hard for the idea but he now has some doubts. His basic notion is that originally the legislative veto was intended as an effective device for congressional oversight. The proper question was not whether regulators were doing a good job but whether they are operating within the limits of the policy laid down by the elected representatives of the people in Congress.

But now when the legislative veto measures are debated in the Congress, the issue is not whether regulators have behaved within the limits set for them, but whether they have behaved wisely and whether the de facto new policy that has been developed is good. Jim O'Hara says that a substantive policy question, debated in the context of a legislative veto vote, does not get the same review and deliberation that a policy matter ought to get. If he is correct, something very pernicious has been added to our governmental system.

CHAIRMAN PERTSCHUK: I think you have really stated, in a far more articulate way, my concerns about the impact of that particular forum on the deliberative process.

SENATOR GRIFFIN: I would add that congressional committees are so busy trying to handle the legislative work that it is hard to imagine how they could adequately review and pass judgment on all of these regulations.

CONGRESSMAN BROWN: If they could not keep up with both regulation and legislative activities perhaps they would have to give up the creation of new legislation. That might be a worthwhile result. [Laughter.]

WALTER BERNS, American Enterprise Institute: The way Dr. Ranney distinguished between legislative oversight and investigation into the wisdom of policy raises real constitutional issues with respect to the one-house veto.

DR. RANNEY: If substantively a one-house veto determines the wisdom of a new policy, in effect one house of Congress is making legislation. That surely is unconstitutional.

PHILIP J. HARTER, attorney and former co-chairman of a presidential task force on OSHA: But if Congress is to review agency regulations doesn't that erode the role of the courts? They are the ones who are supposed to review the actions of regulatory agencies to determine if they comply with legislative intent.

DR. MILLER: I suspect there is no way we can solve all the problems of legislative veto or even of regulation in one session. Thus, I would like to thank our guest, Chairman Pertschuk, for an informative and lively exchange of views. Mike, I hope you will visit with us again soon.

Mr. Pertschuk: I would welcome that, inasmuch as I have very much enjoyed this session.